Taking Action

Working Through PROCRASTINATION and Achieving Your Goals

Jay Earley, PhD

⊞ PATTERN SYSTEM BOOKS

Larkspur, CA

TAKING ACTION:
Working Through Procrastination and Achieving Your Goals

▨ PATTERN SYSTEM BOOKS

140 Marina Vista Ave.
Larkspur, CA 94939
415-924-5256
www.patternsystembooks.com

Paperback ISBN-13: 978-0-9855937-6-6
LCCN: 2012912652

Printed in the United States of America

Introduction to the
Pattern System Series

This is a series of books that are based on the *Pattern System*SM—a comprehensive mapping of the human psyche. You can use the Pattern System to obtain a complete map of your psyche. You will be able to see your strengths and your defenses, your places of pain and how you compensate for them. You'll come to understand the structure of your inner conflicts and see where you are ready to grow. The Pattern System makes clear what you need to explore next in order to resolve the issues that are most important to you.

You'll learn where there is underlying pain, shame, or fear that must be healed. You'll also learn which healthy psychological capacities you can develop (or are already developing) to become happier and more productive.

In the Pattern System, *patterns* represent dysfunctional behaviors that cause problems for us or other people. *Healthy capacities* are the ways we feel and act that make our lives productive, connected, and happy. The Pattern System organizes the patterns and capacities according to various psychological *dimensions,* such as intimacy, power, and self-esteem.

Once you learn the basics of the Pattern System, if you choose to explore more deeply, you'll learn other concepts. At a deeper level are *motivations,* which are the types of intentions underlying your behavior and which are often unconscious. They are derived from the hurtful ways you were treated in childhood, which are represented by *wounds.*

Each book will cover one pattern and the corresponding healthy capacity that is needed to break free of it. In the process of learning about each pattern, you can delve into its motivations and the wounds behind them. This will help you to transform your way of living from the pattern to the capacity.

See http://thepatternsystem.wikispaces.com for an outline and fuller description of the Pattern System.

With the advent of ebooks, there is no longer a need to dispense self-help information in the standard book length (about 300 pages). It is now very easy to create a comprehensive document of any length that is appropriate, without padding or overkill. Each ebook will be short (about 100 pages) while still providing you with the essential information you need to change a troubling psychological pattern and to improve and enhance your life.

Acknowledgments

I am grateful for detailed and helpful suggestions from Anna Rosenhauer, Victoria Smith, Julius Tilvikas, Everett Considine, Bonnie Weiss, and Olive Keating.

I appreciate the sharp eyes and clear mind of Kira Freed, who provided quality editing as well as interior design for the paperback version. As always, I love the clear aesthetic that Jeannene Langford brings to cover design.

Rachel Whalley created the workbook, and Kathy Wilber has done an excellent job on the programming behind it. My virtual assistant, Doreen DeJesus, has been continually in the background, helping with many tasks that keep the work flowing.

Contents

Introduction

Do you find yourself avoiding important tasks? Is it hard for you to make decisions and take action to move your life ahead? When you are faced with a project that must be completed, do you get distracted or busy with other tasks? Is it difficult for you to discipline yourself to exercise, meditate, eat well, or something similar?

If you answered yes to some of these questions, you are one of the many people struggling with Procrastination. You are unconsciously avoiding tasks that must be done. Crucial actions get put off or forgotten. Despite the best of intentions, you can't move ahead with the projects, plans, or actions that are needed for your life to work.

Perhaps you keep putting off a task that needs to be done until the very last minute, and then you pull an all-nighter in order to finish it. You pay the price of stress, lost sleep, and doing a poor job because of the rush to get it finished. Perhaps you perpetually finish assignments or projects late, and you lose the respect of your coworkers, teachers, or boss.

Procrastination can cause serious problems in your work or your studies. It can make it difficult to initiate action to change or advance your life. It can keep you stuck in a quagmire where your life is on hold, leading to hopelessness and depression.

You may be aware of your pattern of Procrastination, but, if you are like most people, you have no idea why this is happening. Consciously, you want to get a task done, or at least you know you need to do it, but somehow it doesn't happen. You may just watch yourself fritter away time and wonder, "What on earth is going on here?"

This book will help you to understand what is behind your Procrastination, and more importantly, it will help you work it through so you can accomplish things. You will be able to move toward whatever has to be done and do it. You'll be able to complete important projects that lead to advancement in your life.

This book can help you set up a discipline for yourself and follow through on it. You will be able to make crucial decisions and take the risks to change your life. Ultimately, you will be able to achieve your goals and dreams.

The Pattern System and Internal Family Systems Therapy

This book is primarily based on the Pattern System (see Introduction to the Pattern System Series). Internal Family Systems Therapy (IFS) is an extremely powerful and user-friendly form of psychotherapy that I use and teach. IFS and the Pattern System complement each other. The Pattern System provides a theory of the psychological content of the human psyche, while IFS provides a powerful method for the healing and transformation of psychological problems.

I have chosen to write this book in such a way that you don't need to understand anything about IFS or parts. For those of you who already know IFS, the concepts in this book are completely compatible with it and can enhance your IFS work on yourself. In Chapter 9, I explain how IFS can be helpful in enhancing the work described in this book.

How to Use This Book

You can use this book to explore either your own Procrastination Pattern or that of another person. The book is written in terms of the reader's pattern, but you can easily apply what you learn to other people. Chapter 2 is for those of you who are reading this specifically to learn about another person.

Visit http://www.personal-growth-programs.com/taking-action-owners to register yourself as an owner of this book, and I will immediately send you an ebook version.[1] As I write subsequent books in this series, I keep noticing improvements I want to make in previous books. If you register as an owner of this book, every time I improve the book, I will email you the latest ebook version. You will also be notified about each new book in the series as it comes out.

---

1. I will send you a Kindle version, which you can read on your computer, tablet, or smartphone using free software that you can download from Amazon.

Even though this book is a workbook, there is also a workbook on the web at http://www.personalgrowth application.com/Pattern/ProcrastinationWorkbook/Pro crastination_Workbook.aspx that goes with this book. There are many places in the book where you can check off items or fill in blanks. You have a choice of doing this directly in this book or using the web workbook instead. All the information in the web workbook will be held under your name and password with complete confidentiality and security. At any point, you will be able to return to the web workbook to look at your answers, change them, or print them out. You will be able to use either workbook to engage in the life practice in Chapter 7.

This book is aimed at helping you change. Therefore, it is crucial that you fill out this workbook or the web workbook and do the practice to change your Procrastination Pattern.

We are forming a Procrastination Online Community of people who are reading this book and would like to support each other in letting go of Procrastination. You can find the Online Community at http://www.personal-growth-programs.com/connect. We will help you find a buddy to talk with as you are reading the book, and especially to help you engage in the life practice in Chapter 7 and to support you in taking action. You can also participate in discussions and phone meetings where you share your struggles and triumphs with others who are dealing with the same issues around Procrastination. The meetings and discussions will be facilitated by myself or a colleague, and we will be available to answer questions of yours that come up.

This support could make all the difference in your success at using this book to work through Procrastination and achieve your goals. It is part of a larger community of people who are working on personal growth and healing through our books, websites, and programs.

Many different patterns are mentioned at various points in this book. Most of these are just for you to explore in more detail if you choose to. If you just want to move ahead to get help with your Procrastination Pattern, feel free to ignore these patterns. It isn't important that you remember or understand them. Just keep reading to get the help you want.

I congratulate you on your willingness to embark on this exciting inner journey. You will soon discover how the Procrastination Pattern operates, the unconscious motives behind it, and where they likely came from in your childhood. You will discover how to transform this pattern so you are free to accomplish what you need to. You will also explore the various aspects of the Work Confidence Capacity and how to cultivate them. And finally, you will have the opportunity to achieve your goals and create the life you want.

CHAPTER 1

Your Procrastination Pattern

If you have a Procrastination Pattern, you tend to avoid certain kinds of action. You may avoid tasks that have to be done that you don't particularly enjoy. You may also avoid things you really want to do, especially activities that involve risks and the possibility of failure. You may start a project but not stay with it or not complete it. Or it may take you so long to finish a task that you miss important deadlines. There may be some arenas in which you procrastinate and others where you don't.

Procrastination usually happens out of awareness. People who procrastinate rarely make a conscious decision not to do something. They just go along with their lives, and after a while they realize that they haven't done the task. They got distracted with other things. They got lost in thought. They spent time online, relaxing, partying, having fun. Sometimes they worked hard doing things that were less important than the task they were avoiding.

Sometimes it isn't a specific task that you are avoiding— it is the thinking and planning that would be required for you to take action. You never seem to find the time to do it. Alternatively, you may think and plan obsessively but never actually make a decision about what action to take.

For example, Angie was tired of her current occupation and wanted to find something that was more creative and meaningful for her. She made lists of interesting lines of work. She thought over different possibilities. She weighed the pros and cons of various directions. But she couldn't make up her mind. There were too many options; she felt confused. Then, for long stretches, she would just get caught up in her current job and life, and forget about her desire for a new career.

As a result of Procrastination, important tasks are left undone or are done late. Projects may be done poorly because they had to be rushed at the last minute. Life decisions are postponed. You may feel stuck in your life because the changes you want to make never quite materialize. Achievement and advancement are put off or abandoned because you don't take the steps to make them happen.

A Story of a Procrastination Pattern

Sandy wanted to take on a creative video project, but she couldn't seem to get started. First she had to clean up her office, and that seemed to take forever. Then she found herself working out on the treadmill. "OK," she thought, "now I'm ready to go." But instead of going to her office, she headed for the kitchen. Half an hour later, she was preparing a three-course meal. After a few days like this, she acknowledged to herself that she was avoiding the project. Sandy had a long-standing pattern of Procrastination, and now it was back.

Once she realized this, she started berating herself for it. A part of her said, "You are such a loser! You should be ashamed of yourself. You never get the important things done. You are going to just waste your life if you don't change." This made Sandy feel terrible about herself. She started feeling down and hopeless.

But she vowed to get going on the project the very next day. And that day, she did start on it and get some preliminary things done. However, the next day she got distracted with some tasks that had to be done and some other tasks that she pretended had to be done, and she didn't do any more work on the video project.

At the end of the day, that critical voice came back in, "There you go again. I am so frustrated with you. You'll never get anywhere with your life. You're worthless."

Naturally, Sandy felt even worse about herself. She felt more depressed, which made her feel low energy and tired. The next day, she didn't even feel like dealing with the video project because it was such a loaded issue, so she just avoided it altogether. In fact, she completely put it out of her mind and forgot about it for about a week. Then the voice came back in and attacked her some more, and she felt bad about herself again. And so the cycle kept repeating.

Procrastination Behaviors and Feelings

The following are common behaviors and feelings that come from the Procrastination Pattern. Which of these apply to you?

- ❐ I avoid taking actions that I know are needed.
- ❐ I have a hard time getting my priorities clear and making decisions.
- ❐ I put off making needed changes in my life.
- ❐ I get stuck in the middle of projects and let them slide.
- ❐ I get distracted and forget about things that have to be done.
- ❐ I avoid doing certain things that involve risk or putting myself out in public.
- ❐ I spend my time thinking, planning, or daydreaming, but I don't actually take action.
- ❐ I spend my time relaxing and enjoying myself rather than doing important tasks.
- ❐ There is something I really want to do, but I never get around to it.
- ❐ When I start a practice of discipline or self-care, I don't stick with it.
- ❐ I miss a deadline for a project at work (or school) or stay up all night to get it finished.
- ❐ I don't carry through on something I have committed to do.

❐ Other behavior _____

_____

❐ Other feelings _____

_____

If you prefer to use a workbook on the web rather than filling out your answers in this book or on paper, visit http://www.personalgrowthapplication.com/Pattern/ProcrastinationWorkbook/Procrastination_Workbook_Behaviors_and_Thoughts.aspx.

You don't have to engage in all these behaviors to have the Procrastination Pattern. And for the ones you do have, you don't have to be doing them all the time.

Your Procrastination Pattern might be operating all the time, or it might be triggered only under certain circumstances, such as when you have an important work work deadline or when you're contemplating a change of direction. Think about the circumstances that tend to trigger your Procrastination.

Procrastination Thoughts

If you listen carefully to your thoughts, you may become aware of ones that are related to Procrastination. Here are some examples. Which ones resonate with you, and in which situations do they tend to come up?

❐ This other job needs to be done first.

❐ I'll take care of it tomorrow.

❐ I don't want to deal with it right now.

❐ I don't like being told what to do.

❒ I don't need to take it on yet.

❒ It's hopeless. I'll never get it done.

❒ I want to have fun.

❒ I need to plan more before I get started.

❒ I can't decide which task is important.

❒ I'm not ready to spend the time it's going to take.

❒ Other behavior _____

_____

❒ Other feelings _____

_____

Situations that Trigger Procrastination

What are typical situations that trigger your Procrastination Pattern? In other words, what do you procrastinate about? For example, projects, health practices, life decisions, making plans, phone calls, routine tasks? List the situations in which you procrastinate. Be very specific—for example, asking a girl out, preparing a speech, writing a proposal, deciding what to throw out, cleaning out the garage. You will process them later in the book.

· making ASEA calls

Types of Procrastination Patterns

There are a number of different kinds of Procrastination Patterns. Check off the ones that are closest to yours.

☐ **Distraction** — do other tasks

You keep yourself busy with tasks other than the one you are avoiding. These tasks may even be ones that need to be done, but you are engaging in them in order to avoid the one task that is the target of your Procrastination. You even make work for yourself that doesn't need to be done—anything to avoid the task you are afraid of.

Instead of doing the task that needs to be done, you get distracted. You read the newspaper or surf the web. You play games to pass the time. You get caught up in a TV show or a novel. You text your friends or watch porn. You take a walk or a nap. You engage in activities that are fun, entertain-

ing, or relaxing, some of which may be fine in themselves, but you are using them to avoid what really must be done.[2]

✓☐ Postponement or Forgetting

You keep telling yourself that you will get to the task tomorrow. Sometimes you have an excuse for putting it off, and sometimes you just postpone it for no good reason. When tomorrow comes, you put it off again—and again. Each time you tell yourself that you will really do it the next day, and you consciously believe that, but the postponement is really an unconscious strategy to avoid the task altogether.

Sometimes you simply forget about a task that is important to do. Then a week or two later, you realize that it hasn't gotten done. You tell yourself that you must do it. Then another week goes by in which you again forget about it. There is a part of you that wants to avoid the task, and it does that by arranging to have you forget about it.

☐ Indecision — *to start the business*

You must take action around a certain issue in your life, but in order to do this, you have to make a decision or set priorities. And you simply can't decide, so the action keeps getting put off. The inability to make the decision can be motivated by a desire to avoid taking the action.

☐ Rebellion

A part of you resents being controlled or told what to do by someone who has assigned you a task or is encouraging

---

2. This may be related to the Eternal Child Pattern (http://www.personal-growth-programs.com/eternal-child-pattern). Follow this link (and those throughout the rest of the book) to see if the books for these patterns are now available.

you to get something done. So you rebel against this person, perhaps unconsciously, by avoiding doing what they want. This is a way of expressing anger, getting back at them, and declaring your autonomy.[3]

Another form of rebellion involves rebelling against the part of you that wants you to do a task. The Defiant part of you perceives the other part as trying to push you or control you, so it refuses to do a task or a discipline that you set up for yourself. This is also a way of expressing anger at the Controlling Part and declaring autonomy. It may seem odd to think that a part of  you might be declaring autonomy from another part of you, but that is often the way it works. This usually goes on unconsciously; all you know is that you have an intention to do something, and it doesn't happen.

Let's look at an example. Jim wanted to start an exercise regime so he would be fitter and lose weight. He created a plan for running on certain days and working out on a weight machine on other days. He did it for a few days, but then the next day he forgot. Then he remembered for a day, and then the next day he didn't feel like doing it, so he put

---

3. In this case, you have the Defiant Pattern (http://www.personal-growth-programs.com/defiant-pattern) as well as the Procrastination Pattern, and they are both involved in the same behavior.

it off. The next day he forgot again, and after that, it didn't happen any more.

A few months later, he decided to try and redouble his efforts to stay on the exercise program, but the same thing happened. He did it for a little while, and then his efforts petered out.

When Jim started exploring this dynamic using the Pattern System, he realized that there was a part of him that felt pushed and controlled by his efforts at exercise. This part of him said, "Don't tell me what to do! You can't control me." So it refused to do the exercise. But all this was happening outside of Jim's awareness until he started exploring it. We will continue Jim's story in Chapter 5.

❏ Harsh Taskmaster Critic

You procrastinate in one of the above ways, and you are harshly judgmental toward yourself about this. There is a part of you that pushes you to do the tasks you are avoiding and criticizes or shames you for not doing them. This is the Taskmaster Pattern.[4] You have an inner conflict or polarization between your Procrastination Pattern and your Taskmaster Pattern, with these two patterns fighting with each other to determine your work habits. (For more information about this, see Chapter 8.) This conflict tears you up inside, and the judgments from your Taskmaster Part make you feel bad about yourself. Yet you continue to avoid doing the tasks that are needed. This is Sandy's situation.

When this happens, most people are only aware of their Taskmaster. Consciously, they want to do the task and feel bad about themselves for not doing it. The part of them that

---

4. http://www.personal-growth-programs.com/taskmaster-pattern

doesn't want to do the task is usually unconscious. This creates an interesting paradox. The part that is conscious and makes all the noise is the Taskmaster, but it doesn't control your behavior. It has the power to make you feel bad, but not the power to make you do the task. For example, Sandy's critical voice (her Taskmaster) made her feel terrible, but it didn't actually get her to do anything. On the other hand, the Procrastinator is silent and hidden, but it is actually in charge. It is in control of your behavior in the sense that it prevents you from doing the task.

This type of Procrastination can be combined with any of the others.

If you would like to take a quiz to help you determine which of these sub-patterns you have, visit http://www. personalgrowthapplication.com/Members/Questionnaire. aspx?Questionnaire=10.

Notice that some of these types are related to other patterns, which you might need to explore to work through your Procrastination. Click on the links in the footnotes to see which of those books are available now.

Please don't feel that you have to remember all the different patterns and capacities that are introduced in this book. Just explore the ones that are relevant for you. The Pattern System will gradually make sense the more you use it. To see an overview of the whole system, read Appendix A or visit http://thepatternsystem.wikispaces.com.

As you read about these patterns that you might have (and others later in the book), please don't judge yourself because you may have some of them. We all have a variety of different patterns of relating that don't work for us. There is nothing deficient or wrong with you because you have some—in fact, just the opposite. You are reading this book because you are interested in learning about yourself and changing your patterns. You are to be congratulated for your commitment to self-awareness.

At this point, if you aren't sure whether you have the Procrastination Pattern or another pattern related to accomplishment, read Chapter 8 and take the quiz on the Accomplishment Dimension. Then if you do have the Procrastination Pattern, return and continue with Chapter 2.

CHAPTER 2

Other People's Patterns

This chapter contains a lot of material condensed into a short space. Take your time reading and reflecting on what is here.

How Your Procrastination Pattern May Affect Your Perception of Other People

If you tend to rebel against other people who give you tasks, you may perceive someone as a hard-driving task-master when they are really just giving you work to do. You might end up procrastinating as a way of getting back at them.

If Someone Close to You Is a Procrastinator

If you suspect that someone close to you has a Procrastination Pattern, you're probably reading this book to try and understand their behavior and feelings. This can be very helpful in getting

clear on where this person is coming from.

In addition, this book can help you understand yourself more deeply. It is possible that you are inadvertently contributing to this person's Procrastination by being pushy, controlling, or judgmental toward them—demanding excessively high levels of work from them and criticizing them for not meeting your standards. Consider whether or not this might be the case before trying to help this person.

You also may be misperceiving someone as a procrastinator because of your overly high standards for work. If you expect too much of a person, you may perceive them as a procrastinator when they are really just working a reasonable amount.

On the other hand, if someone close to you **is** a procrastinator, you might be unconsciously encouraging them by engaging with them in play, distractions, or extraneous busywork when they really need to be dealing with the task they are avoiding. You can help them by simply not participating in their Procrastination.

How to Relate to a Procrastinator

If you are close to someone who procrastinates, there are some things you can do to minimize this tendency in them. Try to avoid triggering this person's fears that lead to Procrastination. Reads Chapter 3 and Chapter 4 to get a sense of which underlying fears this person might have that lead them to procrastinate. Talk with them to get a better sense of what they might be afraid of. This will help you to be aware of times when you unintentionally trigger this person's fears.

For example, if this person is afraid of being controlled or judged with respect to work, be on the lookout for anything you might say that contains any hint of criticism or demand. Even if this person is overly sensitive to judgment or control, you can maximize the chances of him or her feeling safe with you by watching what you say. You can use phrases like, "I'm sure you'll find your own rhythm for what you need" or "I trust that you can set priorities that will work for you" or "I know you're doing your best."

When this person says you are being critical, stop for a moment before you respond. Consider what they are saying and see if you were judgmental. Take them seriously, without being defensive. See if you can become aware of your judgmental behavior in the future. You can even make a point of giving this person compliments about the work they produce and the steps they take, no matter how small.

If this person says that you are being demanding or controlling, consider whether or not this might be true. See if you can become aware of ways that you **expect** them to comply with your desires rather than asking them to. Go out of your way to phrase things as requests rather than demands, and then make sure to be open to the person saying no to your request.

When you make a *request,* it means that if the person refuses, you are OK with that. When you make a *demand,* it means you expect the person to comply or else you will be angry or upset. Work on making only requests and making this clear to the person. This will minimize the changes of their procrastinating.

CHAPTER 3

The Underlying Motivation for Procrastination

Outline of the Change Process

The next five chapters constitute the heart of the change process for Procrastination. Here is an outline:

- Chapters 3 & 4: Understand underlying motivations (mainly fears) for Procrastination and their origins in childhood.

- Chapter 5: Work through these fears so your Procrastination begins to let go.

- Chapter 6: Explore the Work Confidence Capacity that you will develop to replace Procrastination.

- Chapter 7: Engage in a life practice to make this happen.

Motivations for Procrastination

In order to change your Procrastination Pattern, it is very helpful to understand the underlying motivation behind it and its origins in your childhood.

You may procrastinate because you are afraid of being emotionally harmed or rejected if you fail or if you succeed, or you might be rebelling against a person or part of yourself.

Some of your fears might be conscious, but others can be deeply buried. You might even know that there is no real danger if you stop procrastinating, but an unconscious part of you is still afraid of it.

This chapter introduces another concept from the Pattern System. *Motivations* are the underlying reasons behind your patterns—what drives them. Your motivations might involve fears, rebellion, or other intentions.

How to Approach This Information

There is potentially painful material to explore in this chapter and the next one. Take it slowly and make sure that you are OK emotionally. Take a break any time you feel the need. Call a friend to talk about the feelings that are coming up, if that would help you feel supported through this process.

As you read through these motivations and think about the ones that pertain to you, please don't judge yourself. It is common for our Inner Critics to use this information to make us feel bad about ourselves. They tell us that we are really screwed up, that we'll never have success. Don't believe these self-attacks.

Keep in mind that everyone has a host of fears, needs, and other underlying motivations for their behavior. And everyone has had a variety of childhood wounds. We don't all have the same wounds and fears, but we all have plenty of them. It is perfectly normal to have a variety of these issues.

You aren't bad or pathological or inadequate because of the ones you have. If your Inner Critic is beating you up about your fears, let it know that judgment isn't helpful. When you can take in new information from an open place, it helps you to see yourself more clearly.

Adopt an attitude of looking at yourself objectively and compassionately as you explore your motivations and wounds. This approach is enormously helpful in learning about yourself. You had to develop these patterns of defense because of the ways you were wounded when you were very young and vulnerable. They aren't your fault. Appreciate yourself for being interested in delving into this material so you can stop procrastinating.

Motivations

Let's look at the different motivations for Procrastination to see which ones resonate with you. Look over the following to see which ones apply to you. If you aren't sure, read the next chapter for more details about each of these motivations and where they come from in childhood.

Fear of Failure

☐ I am afraid of failing at the task and being judged for this.

☐ I am afraid of failing at the task and being shamed for this.

☐ I am afraid of failing at the task and being rejected for this.

☐ I am afraid of being judged as a failure at the task by a part of me.

Fear of Success

☐ I am afraid of being successful, visible, and powerful, and being attacked for this.

☐ I am afraid of being successful, visible, and powerful, and being rejected for this.

Fear of the Consequences of an Action or a Choice

☐ I am afraid that if I take a certain action or make a choice, I will be judged.

☐ I am afraid that if I take a certain action or make a choice, I will be shamed.

☐ I am afraid that if I take a certain action or make a choice, I will be yelled at or hit.

☐ I am afraid that if I take a certain action or make a choice, I will be rejected.

Avoidance of Unpleasantness

☐ I want to avoid tasks that are boring or unpleasant.[5]

Being the Opposite of a Parent

☐ My mother (or father) was such a workaholic or so perfectionistic that it made my life difficult, so I swore that I would never be like that. I went to the opposite extreme by avoiding work and accomplishment.

Rebelling Against a Person

☐ I am rebelling against a person who pushes me too hard to work.

---

5. This may be related to the Eternal Child Pattern (http://www.personal-growth-programs.com/eternal-child-pattern).

Inner Conflict Between Procrastinator and Taskmaster

☐ I am rebelling against my Taskmaster.

☐ I am rebelling against a part I perceive as a Taskmaster.

☐ I am asserting myself against my Taskmaster.

☑ My Taskmaster and Procrastinator are in conflict.

The next chapter goes into more detail about each of these motivations and their origins in your childhood situation.

CHAPTER 4

Details About Motivations and Childhood Origins

For each type of motivation from the previous chapter, there is a section in this chapter with more detail about that motivation and the childhood situation it comes from or the other patterns that are involved.

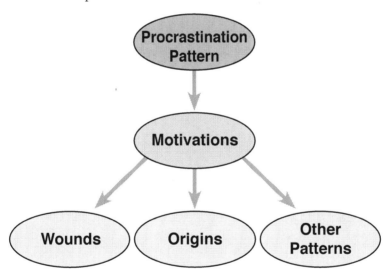

There are a number of different ways to use this chapter.

1. If you already have a pretty good idea about your motivations, you can skip this chapter and perhaps come back to it later to explore where they come from in your childhood.

2. You can go directly to those motivations you checked off in the previous chapter and only explore them.

3. You can read through the entire chapter to get a fuller understanding of your motivations and where they come from. However, if all the detail doesn't feel helpful right now, feel free to skip to the next chapter and come back to this one at a later time.

This chapter introduces two more concepts from the Pattern System. *Wounds* and *origins* are the ways you were treated when you were a child that led to your dysfunctional patterns of behavior as an adult. *Wounds* refer to the pain underlying your motivations, while *origins* refer to the ways your behavior was shaped in childhood.

How to Approach This Material

Caution: There is a lot of detailed and potentially painful material to explore in this chapter. Feel free to stop at any point when you feel you have processed enough for the moment or for today. Take it slowly and make sure that you are OK emotionally. Take a break any time you feel the need. It often helps to process things gradually. When you sit for a while with something difficult, you can digest it more easily, like a big meal. Call a friend or your buddy from the Procrastination Online Community to talk about the feelings that are coming up, if that would help you feel supported through this process.

Many motivations and wounds are named in this chapter. It isn't important that you remember or understand them all—only the ones that are relevant to your Procrastination Pattern. Feel free to ignore the others and just focus on understanding where your Procrastination comes from.

If you have more than one of these motivations and wounds, don't try to process them all at once. Monitor yourself so you can process what you are learning and so you don't get overwhelmed emotionally. Just look at some of them, and come back to the others later.

If two or three of these motivations or wounds seem similar to you, don't worry about teasing them out—just check off all of them. For example, if judgment and rejection seem similar to you, it is probably because you were both judged and rejected. Just check off both of them, and then in Chapter 5, process them together.

Now let's begin with the first motivation.

Fear of Failure

You might be afraid of what will happen if you fail at the task you are avoiding. Of course, some of these things you fear might actually happen if you failed, but your assumption that you will fail comes from your underlying issues, and, of course, avoiding the task is a sure way to fail.

There are four things you might be afraid of, and each is related to a wound. Look them over to see which one fits your Procrastination Pattern. You might have more than one.

☑ Fear of Being Judged for Failing at a Task

You might be afraid of being judged by people if you fail in any way.

This is related to the *Deficiency Wound.* When you were a child, you may have been criticized and made to feel inadequate and like a failure. This criticism may have come from your parents, siblings, or someone else you were close to. You might be afraid of this happening again in your adult life.

☐ Fear of Being Shamed for Failing at a Task

You might be afraid of being shamed or ridiculed by people if you fail in any way.

This is related to the *Shame Wound*. When you were little, you may have been ridiculed, shamed, or embarrassed by parents or others you were close to for failing at something. You might be afraid of this being repeated in your adult life.

☐ Fear of Being Rejected for Failing at a Task

You may be afraid of being rejected by people if you fail in any way.

This is related to the *Unlovable Wound*. When you were a child, your parents, siblings, or friends may have rejected or dismissed you for failing at something, and you ended up feeling unlovable. Now you might fear that if you try to complete tasks, you'll be rejected again.

☐ Fear of Being Judged as a Failure by a Part of Me

You may be afraid of attempting a task and being judged as a failure by a part of you. This part would have either the Taskmaster Pattern[6] or the Perfectionist Pattern.[7]

This is also related to the *Deficiency Wound*, discussed above.

by taskmaster part

---

6. http://personal-growth-programs.com/taskmaster-pattern
7. http://personal-growth-programs.com/perfectionist-pattern

Any of the fears related to failure can be due to a Perfectionist Pattern. You may be so afraid of not doing the task well enough because of the super-high standards of your Perfectionism that you put off starting it. In this case, you may have to work through your Perfectionism before you will be able to stop procrastinating.[8]

Soothing Your Pain

As you read through these descriptions of childhood experiences, painful emotions may come up. It is helpful to soothe yourself when this happens. The best way to do this is to treat each painful emotion as coming from a child part of you—an inner child who was wounded when you were young.

Take a moment to contact this child inside of you. You may see an image of this inner child or feel him or her in your body, or just have a sense of the child. Open your heart to this little being. Be the compassionate, nurturing parent that this wounded inner child needs right now. Listen to his or her pain with caring. Imagine holding this child in your arms. Let the child know that you are there for him or her. Give this inner child the love he or she needs. And give the child whatever else he or she may need—acceptance, validation, encouragement, support, appreciation, and so on. This will keep you from being overwhelmed by the pain that is coming up, and it may even help to heal that wound in you.

To listen to a guided meditation for nurturing this

---

8. See my book *Letting Go of Perfectionism* (http://personal-growth-programs.com/ifs-book/letting-go-of-perfectionism).

wounded inner child, visit http://www.personalgrowth application.com/Pattern/ProcrastinationWorkbook/ Procrastination_Workbook_Inner_Child_Meditation.aspx.

Sandy's Motivation Story

Sandy's Procrastination was motivated by a fear of being shamed, even though Sandy wasn't consciously aware of this. When Sandy was a child, she endured some very painful incidents when she was ridiculed by other kids. Each time this happened, it was because she had done something that made her publicly visible.

For example, once she pushed to the front of a group of girls to get on a carnival ride, and they ridiculed her for this. Another time, she was laughed at for holding hands with a boy she liked. Now whenever she attempts to accomplish something that could make her visible again, such as the video project, this old fear gets triggered, like an echo from her past. Her Procrastination Pattern kicks in, attempting to protect her from being shamed again.

Sandy's story will continue in Chapter 5.

Fear of Success

❏ Fear of Being Attacked for Being Successful, Visible, or Powerful

You might be afraid that if you display your success, good fortune, or positive ability, others will get angry at you for having a big head or being narcissistic. Of course, it is possible that you have really been treated this way by some people, but most likely your concerns are at least partly based on your own underlying issues.

This is related to the *Fear of Anger Wound.* When you were

little, your parents (or others) may have gotten angry at you for "having a swelled head." Now you might be frightened of that happening again if you put effort into shining or standing out. This could also happen if one of your parents got attacked for being successful—for example, excelling beyond what's typical for their race or class and then being targeted for "not knowing their place."

❏ **Fear of Being Rejected for Being Successful, Visible, or Powerful**

You may be afraid that if you display your success, good fortune, or positive ability, others will reject you or abandon you for trying to go beyond where you belong or for leaving them behind. Or you might feel loyal to your parents and not want to progress past what they achieved for fear of losing their love.

This is related to the *Unlovable Wound*. When you were a child, your parents, siblings, or friends may have rejected you for being too successful or visible. Now you might fear that if you go for what you really want, you'll be rejected again.

Fear of the Consequences of an Action or a Choice

You might be afraid of taking a certain action because you expect to be judged, shamed, yelled at, hit, or rejected. For example, you might be afraid of confronting your partner for fear that he will yell at you.

You also might be afraid of making a certain choice because you expect to be hurt in one of those ways. For example, you might be afraid that if you decide to pursue a certain job, you will be shamed in your job interviews. Or you might be afraid of being rejected if you take a certain action, such as calling a girl for a date.

These cases are related to different underlying wounds, depending on your fear. It could come from:

☑ The *Deficient Wound* if you are afraid of being judged

☑ The *Ashamed Wound* if you are afraid of being shamed

☐ The *Afraid of Anger Wound* if you are afraid of being yelled at or hit

☐ The *Unlovable Wound* if you are afraid of being rejected

Avoidance of Unpleasantness

You might avoid tasks that you find boring or unpleasant that need to be done.

This is related to the Eternal Child Pattern,[9] which involves wanting to avoid some of the responsibilities of adulthood.

---

9. http://personal-growth-programs.com/eternal-child-pattern

Being the Opposite of a Parent

Your mother (or father) may have been so ambitious and productive that it made your life difficult, so you swore that you would never be like that. You might have gone to the opposite extreme by avoiding challenges.

Rebelling Against a Person

You might be angry at someone who is pushing you too hard to do certain work or who you feel is demanding and controlling, so you are procrastinating at doing the work in order to rebel against them. For example, your boss may be demanding long hours and giving you no appreciation, so you are avoiding the work to get back at him. This motivation might or might not be conscious.

This is related to the Defiant Pattern,[10] which is a way of asserting your autonomy and preventing people from controlling you.

Inner Conflict Between
Procrastinator and Taskmaster

It is fairly common for Procrastination to be at least partly motivated by a desire to fight against a part of you that is pushing you to work hard. In other words, there are two

---

10. http://personal-growth-programs.com/defiant-pattern

parts of you at war—your Procrastinator and your Task-master. The Taskmaster Pattern[11] involves pushing and demanding long, hard work, and also possibly judging you when you don't meet these standards.

Let's look at four possibilities:

❏ Inner Rebellion Against Your Taskmaster

Your Procrastinator Part might be angry at being controlled by your Taskmaster, so it rebels against this control, just the way you might rebel against another person whom you perceived as trying to control you. This is an attempt to express anger, fight back, and declare your autonomy. It may sound strange to think that one part of you could react this way to another part of you, but this is a fairly common underlying dynamic, and it is almost always unconscious.

This is related to an inner version of the Defiant Pattern,[12] where you defy a part of yourself. It often goes back to a childhood situation in which you were dominated or controlled by a parent. In order to work this through, you may also have to work on your Taskmaster Pattern.

❏ Inner Rebellion Against a Perceived Taskmaster

As in Jim's story from Chapter 1, you might just be trying to get tasks done or engage in a helpful discipline, so you don't really have a Taskmaster Pattern. However, your Procrastinator has a Defiant Pattern and therefore thinks that you have a Taskmaster Part that is trying to control it, so it rebels against this control.

In this case, the Taskmaster isn't the problem—it's your inner Defiant Pattern.

---

11. http://personal-growth-programs.com/taskmaster-pattern
12. http://personal-growth-programs.com/defiant-pattern

❒ **Assertiveness Against a Controlling Taskmaster**

You might have a harsh, dominating Taskmaster, and therefore it makes sense to not give in to its demands for workaholism. When you don't work as hard as your Taskmaster expects you to, it may get demanding and judgmental, and accuse you of Procrastination, among other things such as laziness and worthlessness. However, in this case, you aren't actually procrastinating—you are just choosing to take time for fun, relaxation, family, friends, and other life pursuits. It just looks like Procrastination to your Taskmaster Part.

In this case, your work needs to be on the Taskmaster Pattern.

❒ **Polarization Between Taskmaster and Procrastinator**

You may have a Taskmaster Pattern as well as your Procrastination Pattern. These two parts of you would have very different ideas about how much work you should be doing in a particular situation and so continually get into fights about it. These fights may or may not be conscious. I will use the term *polarization* to describe such an inner conflict between two parts of you. Taken from Internal Family Systems Therapy (IFS), *polarization* means that the two parts of you are not only in conflict, but each believes that it must be extreme to counter what it considers to be the destructive tendencies of the other part.

In the process of these fights, each part becomes angry, stubborn, and disparaging toward the other part. They each become set in their ways. Let's look at an example.

Nancy's Polarization

Nancy had a business making jewelry. Because her business was so successful, she had many orders to fill every day, and her Taskmaster, which she called the Work Ethic Part, was concerned about her working hard enough. It said, "You have to fulfill all the orders you get without too much delay and also take care of all the other aspects of your business. You have to keep your customers happy. I'm really worried about your livelihood given the state of the economy."

However, Nancy found herself slacking off and not really working efficiently. She ended up daydreaming when she was supposed to be working and getting tired and sleepy some of the time. She would stop and wander around her yard for a while instead of getting work done.

At first she didn't know why this was happening, but when she began to explore herself using the Pattern System and IFS, she learned that the slacking off came from her Procrastinator Part. It said, "I feel completely stifled by all this work. I need time for relaxation and creativity. Your life of constant work feels very dull and boring." It wasn't simply a Procrastinator—it was also her artistic and fun-loving part.

Her Work Ethic Part said, "I'm afraid that if I gave you time for fun and creativity, you wouldn't get enough work done." Her Procrastinator Part said, "If I don't forcibly take time off by daydreaming, the Work Ethic Part would have you working all the time." The two parts really didn't trust each other at all.

You can see that this wasn't simply a matter of unnecessary Procrastination or an overly harsh Taskmaster. Each side had reasonable desires for Nancy and important wisdom for her. She did need to run her business well and take care of her financial well-being. She also needed free time to enjoy life. Nancy had a well-developed creative side; that's one reason she was successful as a jewelry maker. And she needed time to wander in her beautiful backyard and enjoy nature, to putter in her garden, and to allow her artistic mind to float free.

The problem wasn't that either side was wrong. It was that they were fighting each other instead of cooperating to find a solution that would work for both of Nancy's needs. Of course, Nancy had no recourse until she became aware of this unconscious fight that was occurring in her psyche.

Nancy's story will continue in the next chapter.

Next Step

Whew! All of this chapter may have been hard to read. Yet it was necessary in order to come to an understanding of what motivates your Procrastination and where this tendency comes from in your past. This will be helpful in changing this pattern.

You should now have a pretty good idea of your motivations for procrastinating. Take your time and get emotional support to process these insights. It can be a lot to take on.

You are now prepared to change your Procrastination behavior, which starts in the next chapter.

My procrastinator's intention/motivations
- don't allow me to start my business
- fear that I won't do well
- fear that I will be reminded that I'm not capable
- wants to protect me from feeling inadequate; not enough; not able

CHAPTER 5

Working Through
Procrastination Fears

N ow that you know which of your underlying fears are
creating Procrastination, let's work them through so
you can accomplish the tasks you want by developing the
Work Confidence Capacity (see Chapter 6).

When a particular task needs to be done, your Procrastination Pattern may become activated. This pattern developed in childhood because you were dealing with a dan-
gerous and harmful situation, for example, being ridiculed
when you tried to get attention or being told that your work
was never good enough. And unconsciously, you believe
this is going to happen again.

However, your current situation is very different from
what happened back then. You are no longer vulnerable
and dependent like a child. You are autonomous and no
longer subject to the power of your parents. You have many
strengths and capacities now as an adult (and possibly because of previous work you have done on yourself) that you
didn't have as a child.

For example, you may be more grounded and centered. You may be able to assert yourself, be perceptive about interpersonal situations, support yourself financially, and so on. You have already accomplished many things in your life and have overcome various obstacles. You are an adult with a much greater ability to handle yourself. You probably have friends, maybe a spouse or lover, perhaps a community you belong to, a support group, professionals you can rely on. You have people you can turn to if necessary.

This means that you aren't in danger the way you were as a child, and your mature self is available, which wasn't possible when you were young. Therefore, it isn't really necessary for you to procrastinate any longer because this is a reaction to past hurts and dangers.

In this chapter, you can work through the fears that lead to Procrastination. You can do this for any particular task or situation that leads to Procrastination. Choose one specific action or situation and apply the rest of this chapter to it. Then when you are finished with that situation, if you want, you can come back to this chapter and choose a different situation to process. I will call this your *Life Situation* because you are targeting it in this chapter.

Are Your Fears Realistic?

First we will consider whether or not your fears or perceptions are accurate. Are the things you are afraid will happen if you take action in this Life Situation really likely to happen? For example, if you are afraid of failing and being shamed, consider whether there is someone who would really shame you. If you are afraid of succeeding and being ostracized by your friends, consider whether your friends would really do that.

These questions aren't always easy to answer without bias. Consider them when you aren't emotionally triggered. Keep in mind that even though there may be a part of you that believes you will be harmed or rejected, this may not actually be the case. You might want to discuss this question with friends who know your situation.

If Your Fear Isn't Realistic

If you decide that you won't be harmed or rejected if you take action in this Life Situation, this indicates that it is really safe for you to take the action or make the decision. What do you know about the life situation that makes your fear unrealistic?

_____

_____

_____

_____

_____

Working Through Sandy's Fears

As an example, let's continue with Sandy's story. Once Sandy realized she was avoiding her video project, she saw that she needed to understand her Procrastination Pattern better. When she explored the pattern, she found that she was trying to avoid feeling shame by never working on something that she might fail at.

Thinking more deeply about it, Sandy discovered that making this video represented a lifelong dream for her. She was frightened that actually working on it would dash her fantasy of being a successful film director. Her unconscious thought process went as follows: "As long as I don't actually start working on this, I could still potentially be awesome at it. But if I do work on it, I might get ridiculed publicly, which would be horrible."

Sandy reminded herself, "I'm not going to be shamed if I show my completed video project to people. Even if my work isn't great, I can learn from the experience and get helpful feedback from viewers so that I can improve."

She reminded herself, "Every creative project builds upon the last one, and I just need to get started."

She was still afraid of that critical Taskmaster Part of her, but she figured, "If I actually do the work, this part will probably stop attacking me." This was enough to get her Procrastination Pattern to let go and allow her to make some headway with her video project.

Sandy's story continues in Chapter 6.

Working Through Jim's Fears

Recall Jim, who kept trying to stay with an exercise program, but a rebellious part of him refused to do it. When he explored this dynamic, he remembered how controlling his father had been and how much he resented this. The Defiant Pattern[13] in Jim was reacting to Jim's wanting to exercise as if Jim were his father.

Once Jim realized this, he sat down and had a talk with his Defiant Part. He explained to this part why he wanted to exercise and the benefits he wanted to get from exercising. "I would like to be in better shape so I can play soccer without getting so winded. I also want to lose 15 pounds so I'll be more attractive to women."

Instead of just setting up the regime, he asked the Defiant Part, "What do you think? Would it be worth doing the exercise in order to be better at soccer and have more attractive women interested in me?" The Defiant Part agreed. As a result of this discussion, the part didn't feel that Jim was being controlling, but rather that Jim and the part had come to a mutual decision about the best action to take. This way the Defiant Part could stop making him procrastinate because it no longer felt that it had to fight for its autonomy.

If Your Fear Is Realistic

Even though your current situation is probably not as harmful as the childhood situation that produced your underlying fears, there may be some degree of validity to your fears. If this is the case, you want to separate out those fears and perceptions that are accurate from those that are not.

If there is some validity to your fear, take a moment to get in touch with exactly what you are afraid will happen if you take action in this Life Situation. Are you afraid your

---

13. http://personal-growth-programs.com/defiant-pattern

teacher will judge you? Are you afraid that you will fail at the task and feel bad about yourself? Write what you are afraid will happen here:

_____

_____

_____

_____

Creating a Plan for This Fear

Make a plan for how you will handle the situation so that either the problems related to your fear won't happen or you will protect yourself if they do.

Here are some possibilities:

1. You will assert yourself in such a way as to keep yourself from being emotionally harmed. For example, if someone tells you that your ideas are stupid, your plan will be to take a moment and think through whether or not you agree. If you don't, you will tell this person that you don't agree and explain why not.[14]

2. You will act in such a way as to maximize your chances of getting the response you want from people. For example, if you need to tell someone that you didn't like the way they treated you, you will do this in a calm way that isn't likely to trigger an angry response.

3. You will set limits that will prevent emotional harm. For example, if someone makes fun of your work,

---

14. You may need to work on developing your Assertiveness Capacity (http://www.personal-growth-programs.com/people-pleasing-pattern) to succeed at this.

you'll tell him that ridiculing you is inappropriate and demand that he stop.[15]

4. You will sit down and talk with the person about changing his or her behavior so you aren't emotionally harmed or rejected. Do this at a time when you aren't in the middle of a conflict with this person. Explain how you are being hurt and make a request for the person to respond differently. Volunteer to listen to their concerns as well.[16]

Work out this plan and write it here:

_____

_____

_____

_____

Then put it into operation and keep a record of your results. You may need to work through one of your patterns or develop a certain capacity for your plan to achieve the success you are looking for. Be aware that it may take time for the plan to succeed. Chapter 7 contains a practice to stop procrastinating and take action that involves using your plan to make this safe.

---

15. You may need to work on developing your Limit-Setting Capacity (http://www.personal-growth-programs.com/limit-setting-capacity) for this plan to succeed.
16. You may need to work on developing your Challenge Capacity (http://www.personal-growth-programs.com/conflict-avoiding-pattern) and Good Communication Capacity (http://www.personal-growth-programs.com/blaming-pattern) to have a successful conversation.

Keep in mind that your fears may be partially realistic and partially not. In that case, you will need to adopt a strategy that is a mix of these two sections.

Working Through Polarization

As discussed at the end of the last chapter, sometimes more is needed than working through your fears that lead to Procrastination. You may have an inner conflict or polarization between your Procrastinator Part and a Taskmaster Part.

In this case, check inside to see what these two parts are and what each of them wants for you. Give them each some space to stake out their positions and speak their minds so you can understand the inner conflict that is resulting in Procrastination.

As an example, let's look again at Nancy's situation. Her Work Ethic Part was afraid that if it gave Nancy time for fun and creativity, she wouldn't get enough work done. Her Procrastinator Part was afraid that if it didn't forcibly take time off by daydreaming, the Work Ethic Part would have her working all the time.

Once each side has spoken up and your understand them, work on getting the two sides to realize that they can each get what they want for you by learning to cooperate rather than by fighting. You need to work out a solution that works for both of them and see if they agree.

Nancy worked out a schedule that involved working during certain hours of the day and consciously taking time off the rest of the time. That way, there wouldn't be a need to steal time by procrastinating because she would have the playtime built in. But she would also schedule enough time to get all the jewelry work done. This was a good start, but her Work Ethic Part was concerned that there was so much extra business-related work that had to be done that she wouldn't have time for this.

So she decided to experiment with that schedule to see if it left her enough time for the other business work. If it didn't, she would think through some larger issues about how she needs to change the way she has set up her business. This was something that both parts could agree to.

IFS has a very effective method for working through polarizations like this, which is described in my book *Resolving Inner Conflict*.[17] In fact, Chapter 11 in that book contains a detailed transcript of a polarization session that Nancy did with these parts. You also might want to take an IFS Course or work with an IFS therapist. See Appendix C for resources.

CHAPTER 6

The Work Confidence Capacity

The Work Confidence Capacity involves the ability to accomplish tasks efficiently but without stress or pressure and with room for relaxation, play, and fun. You have confidence that you can do tasks well and be successful in your endeavors. You can keep track of things you need to do, stay focused, and set priorities. You can make decisions about your goals and the larger direction of your life.

Look over the aspects of Work Confidence below and check the ones you would like to develop.

Aspects

- ❐ Courage to work on task
- ❐ Feeling capable of getting my work done
- ❐ Confidence that I can be successful

❒ Trusting my ability to achieve my goals

❒ Appreciating each step I take

❒ Being in the flow of my creative process

❒ Keeping track of all the important details

❒ Keeping track of what needs to be done and acting on it

❒ Staying with a discipline, even when it gets hard

❒ Setting priorities about what task to do at any give time

❒ Being decisive

❒ Staying focused

❒ Being able to meet my deadlines with ease

❒ Producing excellent work

❒ Balancing relaxation, play, and enjoyment with getting the task done

❒ Other aspects_____

_____

A Story of Developing the Work Confidence Capacity

Sandy started to practice evoking Work Confidence, reminding herself of all the video classes she had taken and reviewing smaller video projects she had done that she liked. She also looked up some motivational quotes to help her realize that she didn't have to be amazing right out of the gate; instead, she could practice and learn, and improve gradually.

She made a point of paying attention to her choices about how she spent her time. When she noticed that she was about to choose a distracting activity rather than working on her project, she reminded herself that she really wanted to do the project.

She told herself, "I have the skills, and I'm actually excited about getting behind the camera." This allowed her to do regular work on the project for the first time.

Once she was accomplishing things, her Taskmaster stopped attacking her. She was doing what it wanted, so it became quiet. This also helped her to feel better about herself and more confident in her abilities because she wasn't being put down and shamed any more.

Sandy's sense of being capable increased with practice, and her attitude toward her video project gradually changed. She began to feel eager to get to it each day, and she spent longer and longer hours with it. She felt happy to be in the creative flow.

Higher Accomplishment

In the Pattern System, in addition to healthy capacities, there are higher capacities, which are the more evolved or spiritual aspects of capacities. When you are living from a higher capacity, you embody a version of the capacity that is less egocentric and more oriented toward the good of the whole. You are living from a place that is informed by the sense that we are all connected and you care for this larger unity.

The Higher Accomplishment Capacity is an integration of the higher aspects of Ease and Work Confidence. It has the following aspects:

Process Is Fulfilling

Your work flows naturally because you aren't attached to its outcome. You are passionate about your work for its own sake. The process is what is important. You are so fully engaged in the process that it is fulfilling in itself, so the work just flows effortlessly.

Which of theses aspects would you like to develop more?

❐ Work flowing easily and naturally

❐ Lack of attachment to outcome of projects

❐ Passion about the work for its own sake

❐ Feeling fulfilled by the process independent of the outcome

Life Purpose

You are committed to excellent work, but not because you care about being successful and admired. Your work has a higher purpose—your calling in life to contribute to the betterment of other people, the environment, or society. You feel passionate about bringing your gifts to the world and making a difference.

Which of theses aspects would you like to develop more?

❐ Having a sense of life purpose

❐ Feeling passionate about bringing my gifts to the world

Flowing with the Universe

You are in touch with the flow of the universe, and you participate in it, cocreating it and following it at the same time. You plan for the future, but you recognize that your plans may have to change according to circumstances, feedback, and your arising sense of what is called for, so you are open to changing your strategies at any moment. When plans aren't necessary, you are able to flow with each moment, taking the action that is needed according to the situation and your deeper sense of purpose.

Which of these aspects would you like to develop more?

❐ Ability to change plans according to new information

❐ Ability to flow with each moment

CHAPTER 7

Practicing Behavior Change

This chapter presents "real-time" practice where you can work on evoking your Work Confidence Capacity to replace your Procrastination Pattern.

This is where the rubber meets the road! This is the practice that can change your Procrastination, and we have provided lots of support for you to make this happen, including the web workbook[17] and the Procrastination Online Community.[18]

Practice Outline

Here is a brief outline of the steps in this chapter:

1. Know why you want to do this practice.

2. Choose a Life Situation to practice on.

3. Know when your Procrastination gets triggered.

4. Remind yourself that Procrastination isn't necessary.

5. Create Work Confidence.

6. Get support for your practice.

7. Track and improve your practice.

17. http://www.personalgrowthapplication.com/Pattern/Procrastina
tionWorkbook/Procrastination_Workbook.aspx
18. http://www.personal-growth-programs.com/connect

Clarifying Your Intention for Doing the Practice

Before you engage in this practice, it is helpful to clearly have in mind what you intend to gain by making this change. It is not enough to just decide that it would be a good thing to do. Figure out why you want to do it, set an intention for your practice, and keep this in mind during the week. This will help you discipline yourself to stick to the practice.

Think through the pain and difficulties caused by your Procrastination Pattern.

Notice those that will motivate you to change:

❐ I'm tired of feeling worthless.

❐ I don't like feeling guilty about turning things in late.

❐ I want to feel good about my capabilities.

❐ I am tired of disappointing myself and others.

❐ I don't like feeling frantic trying to get things done at the last minute.

❐ I want to complete what I start.

❐ I am tired of my Taskmaster berating me for not doing things.

❐ Other pain and difficulties _____

_____

_____

What do you have to gain from living from Work Confidence Capacity in your life, especially those things you really want?

- ❐ Feeling confident
- ❐ Being respected by colleagues and friends
- ❐ Feeling capable
- ❐ Feeling proud of myself
- ❐ Taking pride in my work
- ❐ Feeling free and unstressed
- ❐ Knowing that I'm making a difference
- ❐ Feeling good about contributing to the world
- ❐ Other things to gain _____

_____

_____

Planning Ahead

Think of a situation that is coming up in the next week or so, or one that arises frequently, in which you want to practice the Work Confidence Capacity. Or instead, think of a situation in which you typically procrastinate and would like to change that. For example:

- I am close to missing an important deadline at work because I just can't get motivated.
- I get distracted whenever it's time to do my bills.
- I can never find the time to make certain phone calls.
- I go blank when I try to think about the next steps in a certain project.

Let's call this the *Life Situation.* If you aren't sure when your Procrastination Pattern gets triggered or if it seems to be around a lot of the time, then leave the Life Situation blank and work on noticing **whenever** that pattern is activated.

As you read through the rest of this chapter, fill in your answers here or in the web workbook. The web workbook will produce a report page that tells you what you plan to do during your life to engage in this practice. You can carry this page of the web workbook with you by printing it out or keeping it on a mobile device.

You can do this practice more than once if you want to work on more than one Life Situation. You will have a different Workbook report page for each practice. If this Life Situation isn't going to come up in the next few weeks, you can do this practice by **imagining** it coming up and how you will change your behavior.

What are you afraid of in this Life Situation? For example, if you've made a commitment to give a public presentation, you might avoid preparing for it because you're extremely anxious that certain people will be angry at you if you do well.

You may have a few specific aspects of Work Confidence that you want to develop in this Life Situation. For example, you might want to develop your ability to believe in your speaking skills and trust that you know the content inside and out. What aspects of Work Confidence do you want to develop in this Life Situation?

Set an intention to pay close attention during the Life Situation to see if your Procrastination Pattern is activated, and be prepared to practice these aspects of Work Confidence instead.

What are the feelings, thoughts, or behaviors that will cue you that your Procrastination Pattern is activated? For example, "I got distracted by something that's a low priority" or "I don't feel like it" or "I start daydreaming" or "It's not that important anyway."

Remember the target fear for this Life Situation. To the extent that it isn't true, what is true instead? What are some statements that will remind you that your target fear won't really happen or that your negative perception isn't accurate? Choose from among the following statements, or create your own:

❐ I will be OK if I go ahead with my work.

❐ Nothing bad is going to happen if I finish my project.

❐ I can handle the next steps once my work is complete.

❐ No one will ridicule me for how I've done my work.

☐ My work is plenty good enough.

☐ I will not get overwhelmed by this work.

☐ Other statements _____

_____

_____

If there is some validity to your fears or perceptions, re-member the plan you devised in Chapter 5 to handle that situation. You will put that plan into action this week.

Creating Work Confidence

Which of these statements will encourage you to create the aspects of Work Confidence you want in this Life Situation?

☐ I can do this work gradually and with ease.

☐ I trust that I can find my own rhythm for getting things done.

☐ I'll be okay if I take it one step at a time.

☐ I can handle it if my work is not perfect.

☐ The more I work on things, the better my ability will get.

☐ Believing in myself will help me produce better work.

☐ I can work competently and successfully.

☐ I can accomplish what I set out to do.

☐ Other statements _____

_____

_____

You can develop an aspect of yourself that I call the Inner Champion, which supports you in being yourself and feeling good about yourself despite your fears. Your Work Confidence Inner Champion encourages you to feel confident in your ability to accomplish what you want without fear.

Visit http://www.personalgrowthapplication.com/Pattern/ProcrastinationWorkbook/Procrastination_Workbook_Meditation.aspx to do a guided meditation to access your Work Confidence Inner Champion.

Which of the following statements would you like your Work Confidence Inner Champion to say to you?

❒ You can do it.

❒ I believe in you.

❒ You are capable.

❒ You can complete this project.

❒ You can do a good job.

❒ You are smart and creative enough.

❒ You can find a way to make this project work.

❒ Each small step gets you closer to your goal.

❒ You can use the feedback you get to improve what you are doing.

❒ There is no reason you can't succeed.

❒ You can learn from any setbacks so you can always move forward.

❒ Other statements _____

_____

_____

What body sensation, feeling, or state of consciousness will help you evoke these aspects of Work Confidence (for example, that sense of self-confidence when you know you are up to the task at hand)? _____

_____

_____

_____

What image will help create Work Confidence (for example, smiling at yourself in a mirror after a success)? _____

_____

_____

_____

Can any people close to you help you create Work Confidence? What help do you want from them (for example, to remind you how great you felt after a past success)?

_____

_____

_____

Is there something you want people close to you to stop doing (for example, telling you to "just do it" when your Procrastination gets triggered)? _____

_____

_____

Talk to the people close to you about what they can do (or stop doing) that will help you activate the Work Confidence Capacity and especially the aspects of Work Confidence you want in this Life Situation.

Your Work Confidence Practice Workbook Section
There is a separate section of the web workbook for helping you engage in your Work Confidence Practice and keep track of it. The rest of this chapter explains how to engage in this practice and use this section.

Working with a Buddy
People have much more success with practices like this if they have a "buddy" to witness them and be their cheerleader. I recommend that you find a friend who is a good listener and who will understand what you are doing and

be supportive. Or join our Procrastination Online Community,[19] where we will help you find a buddy.

After you make your plans for the practice, call your buddy and talk through what you will be doing. If you have written down specific words you want to say in the situation, practice saying them to your buddy. Even role-play the situation. Have your buddy play your boss or a coworker while you practice interacting with him or her in a way that would create the work confidence you want.

Set a time frame for checking in with your buddy on your progress with the practice. You could just do it once at the end of a week to report on how the practice has gone. But for even more effective support, consider checking in with your buddy every two or three days, or even every day, to let him or her know how it is going. The act of reporting in will really help to keep you on track. When you know that you'll be talking to someone about your practice, you're much more likely to do it and to keep track of what happened.

Your Buddy can also support you in doing tasks or taking actions that you have been avoiding. You can share with your Buddy the things you want to do, knowing that you will be talking to him or her about whether or not you did them. This can be crucial support for your being accountable for your action plans and following through on them.

When the Life Situation Occurs

With some Life Situations, you know ahead of time when they will happen. For example, you know when you will be

---

19. http://www.personal-growth-programs.com/connect

preparing to make a phone call to scout out a new opportunity. In these cases, take some time right before this happens to go to Work Confidence Practice Plans[20] in the web
workbook (or review the pages in the paperback workbook)
to review how you want to handle this Life Situation. (Keep
in mind that the web workbook and the Profile Program are
two different programs.) If you don't have time right before
it happens, take some time earlier to prepare.

Some situations allow you to process this material **during**
the Life Situation. For example, if the Life Situation involves
preparing for a presentation, you can take a time-out from
the preparation, process the Procrastination feelings that are
coming up, and then return to your work and put your plan
into operation. In this case, when you take the time-out,
click the above two links to review how you plan to handle
the situation so you can decide what to do.

During the life situation, pay close attention and notice
the feelings, thoughts, or behaviors that will cue you that
your Procrastination Pattern is activated.

If it is triggered, do the following:

- Say the statements (out loud or silently) that will remind you that you don't have to be afraid of Work
Confidence, or create your own on the spot.

- Put your plan into action to assert yourself around the
possibility of judgment, shame, failure, or rejection.

20. http://www.personalgrowthapplication.com/Pattern/Procras
tinationWorkbook/Procrastination_Workbook_Practice_Plans.aspx?
pname=LifeSituation

- Say the statements (out loud or silently) that will inspire you to create Work Confidence, or create your own on the spot.

- Use a body sensation, feeling, or state of consciousness (if you have chosen one) to help create Work Confidence.

- Look at the image you have chosen (if you have one) to inspire you to create Work Confidence.

If you were successful in creating Work Confidence, celebrate your success! Give yourself a pat on the back or a reward, such a fun afternoon outing. Appreciate yourself for this step in changing your behavior. It is very important to reinforce each step, however small, in the right direction.

After the situation has happened, enter your Practice Notes (see below) as soon as you have time to enter what happened. Or if you don't have time, do it at the end of the day when doing your Daily Check-In Notes.

If you came up with new statements, add them to your workbook to use in the future. If you have additional insights into any of the material you have filled out previously in the workbook, feel free to add them to the pages you have already filled out.

Practice Notes

Enter your answers according to what you did in your practice. (Not all need to be answered.)

The Life Situation _____

_____

_____

The fears that came up in this situation _____

_____

_____

The aspects of Work Confidence you were working on developing in this situation _____

_____

_____

What triggered the Procrastination Pattern _____

_____

_____

The statements you said to remind yourself that you don't have to be afraid of Work Confidence _____

_____

_____

_____

What you did to assert yourself to handle judgment, shame, failure, or rejection _____

_____

_____

_____

The statements you said to yourself to inspire you to create Work Confidence _____

_____

_____

The body sensation, feeling, or state of consciousness you used to help create Work Confidence _____

_____

_____

The image you used to inspire you to create Work Confidence _____

_____

_____

How you did in attempting to create Work Confidence

_____

_____

_____

Further notes on what happened _____

_____

_____

_____

Is there anything you want to do differently next time?

_____

_____

_____

Daily Check-In

In order to remember to do this practice, it will help you to check in with yourself once a day in addition to any checking in with your friend. Choose a time when you will have a few minutes to yourself and when it will be easy for you to remember to check in each day. For many people, this is right before going to bed each night or upon waking each morning. But in all cases, choose a consistent time of day that works best for you.

If the Life Situation only occurs once a week or a few times a month, you don't need to enter Daily Check-In Notes every day. Just reflect to see if it happened that day and take notes if it did. On the days it didn't happen, you don't need to do anything.

Take notes on what you were aware of that day. If the Life Situation occurred, write down what happened. Enter these below.

Reflect on whether the Procrastination Pattern was activated today, whether you noticed and did the practice, and what happened. _____

_____

_____

Did the Life Situation happen today? _____

_____

_____

If so, were you paying attention when it happened? _____

_____

Did the Procrastination Pattern get triggered today (in that situation or any other one)? _____

If so, did you notice when the Procrastination Pattern was triggered today? _____

If you didn't, what kept you from noticing? _____

_____

_____

_____

What can you do tomorrow to help you be more aware?

_____

_____

_____

If you did notice that the Procrastination Pattern was triggered, did you do the practice to evoke Work Confidence?

_____

If not, what stopped you from doing that? _____

_____

_____

What can you do next time to help yourself remember to evoke Work Confidence? _____

_____

_____

If you did the practice and didn't track what happened at the time, enter it under Practice Notes. If you did it more than once, take separate notes for each instance by clicking that link multiple times.

Is there anything you want to do differently tomorrow or the next time your Procrastination Pattern is triggered?

_____

_____

_____

Weekly Check-In

After a week, take notes on how this practice is working.

Day of week _____

How many times did you do the practice this week? _____

Was this enough to be helpful to you? _____

If you did the practice enough, how much of a difference

did it make? _____

_____

What worked in doing the practice? _____

_____

_____

_____

What didn't work in doing the practice? _____

_____

_____

_____

Do you want to do the practice again next week? _____

Is there anything you want to do differently next week?

_____

_____

_____

CHAPTER 8

The Accomplishment Dimension

The information in this chapter will help you to get a fuller sense of the various patterns and healthy capacities you might have with respect to accomplishment. You might learn about other patterns you want to explore and may see the relationships between your patterns and capacities. However, if you aren't interested in this level of complexity, feel free to skip this chapter or come back to it at a later time.

The Accomplishment Dimension

The Procrastination Pattern is part of the *Accomplishment Dimension* in the Pattern System. Let's look at how it is related to the other patterns and capacities.

There are five problematic interpersonal patterns in the Accomplishment Dimension—Taskmaster, Procrastination, Resigned, Perfectionist, and Sloppy.[21]

- The **Taskmaster Pattern** involves pushing yourself unmercifully to overwork, often in an attempt to be very successful, and judging yourself harshly whenever you don't.

---

21. There will be books on most of these patterns. Visit http://personal-growth-programs.com/pattern-system/pattern-system-series to see if they are available.

- The **Procrastination Pattern,** as discussed previously, involves avoiding tasks that need to be done.

- The **Resigned Pattern** involves not having confidence that you can accomplish your goals or get anywhere in life and therefore not trying to do anything or be anything.

- The **Perfectionist Pattern** involves believing you must always do everything perfectly and that it's never OK to make a mistake.

- The **Sloppy Pattern** involves caring very little about your work and appearance, doing as little as possible, and having low standards.

Two healthy capacities—Ease and Work Confidence—are related to these five patterns.

- **Ease** is the ability to accomplish tasks in a relaxed, easy way without stress or striving.

- **Work Confidence,** as discussed previously, is about being confident and able to work well, accomplish tasks, and produce excellent work, with deep caring and devotion for what you produce, and taking pride in the great work you create.

Work Confidence is a complement to Ease. For healthy accomplishment, you need both capacities. Ease helps you to relax and your work to flow, and with Work Confidence, you feel strong about your gifts and your ability to be productive on the job. If you have Work Confidence, you easily engage in tasks that need to be done. You are clear and careful in your work and can work hard to achieve your goals, but without overstriving.

This is the nature of healthy capacities—they naturally integrate with each other, which means that they don't oppose each other. They work together; they both support your flourishing in achievement-related ar-eas of your life. If you have both capacities, you are able to relax while at the same time being confident that you can successfully apply yourself when called for.

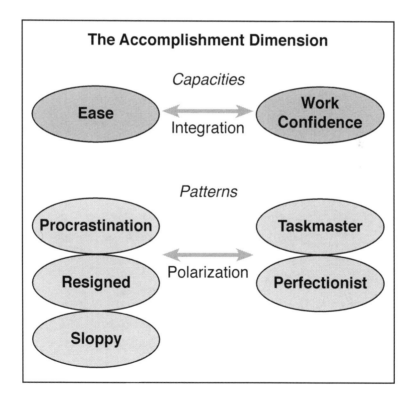

The Accomplishment Dimension

Capacities

Ease ⟷ Integration ⟷ Work Confidence

Patterns

Procrastination   Taskmaster

Resigned ⟷ Polarization ⟷ Perfectionist

Sloppy

Relations Between the Patterns and Capacities

Patterns in Conflict

The patterns on the left and right sides don't integrate with each other in the way the healthy capacities do. They are polarized, which means they battle each other to determine how you get tasks done. On the one hand, the Procrastination Pattern involves avoiding doing work, and the Resigned Pattern involves having no initiative. On the other hand, the Taskmaster Pattern involves driving yourself unnecessarily hard with intense striving and beating yourself up for not working hard enough.

The Sloppy Pattern involves doing poor work and having little to no investment in doing something well, while the Perfectionist Pattern involves an unhealthy obsession with doing things perfectly and judging yourself as never good enough. Another way to look at it is that the three patterns on the left are about *under*functioning, while the two on the right are about *over*functioning.

You might be driven with certain tasks and avoid others. Perhaps you avoid taking on a project for fear of becoming too driven or perfectionistic if you did.

In some cases, paradoxically, a Perfectionist (or Taskmaster) Pattern can actually lead to a lack of Work Confidence. You might have such high standards for achievement or perfection that you feel inadequate because you can never meet them.

Patterns Are Dysfunctional Versions of Capacities

Ease is a healthy version of the Procrastination, Resigned, and Sloppy Patterns. Another way to say this is that those three patterns are extreme, dysfunctional versions of Ease.

They are attempts to feel okay by staying away from work that could be criticized, or to attain relaxation and fun by avoiding work or being apathetic about achievement.

The same applies on the right side. Work Confidence is a healthy version of the Taskmaster and the Perfectionist. Or you can say that the Taskmaster and Perfectionist Patterns are extreme, dysfunctional versions of Work Confidence. The Taskmaster and Perfectionist Patterns try to make you work hard and be successful and perfect by pushing and judging you.

Capacities Resolve Patterns

If you have the Procrastination, Resigned, or Sloppy Patterns, Work Confidence is what you need to develop to break away from them. That's why Work Confidence is emphasized in this book on Procrastination. Thus the capacity on the opposite side of the graphic is the one needed to transform a pattern. In order to get there, you will need the courage to face and work through your fears, develop confidence in your talents and abilities, practice follow-through, and apply yourself to achieve goals.

The same applies on the other side. If you have a Taskmaster Pattern or Perfectionist Pattern, you need Ease to break free from it. When you develop a sense of ease, you'll trust that you can accomplish your goals without driving yourself all the time.

Here is another graphic showing these relationships:

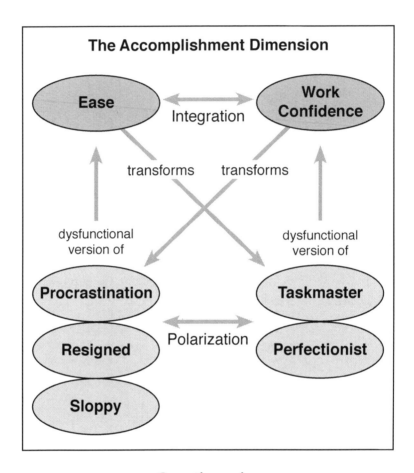

Questionnaire

It would be helpful to track which of the patterns and capacities in this dimension you have. You may have an idea from reading the descriptions, or you can take a quiz on our website. This questionnaire will give you a score for each of the patterns and capacities in the Accomplishment Dimension to help clarify how strongly you have the Procrastination Pattern or each of the other patterns in that dimension. It will also tell you how high you score on the healthy capacities in that dimension. To take this quiz, visit http://www.personalgrowthapplication.com/Members/Questionnaire.aspx?Questionnaire=10.

CHAPTER 9

Conclusion

Deep Healing and Transformation of the Procrastination Pattern

When I do psychotherapy with my clients, I use Internal Family Systems Therapy (IFS), a very powerful, cutting-edge approach developed by pioneering psychologist Richard Schwartz, PhD. Since I discovered IFS a decade ago, I have seen amazing results in my clients' lives. I was developing the Pattern System for more than a decade before I discovered IFS and was thrilled to find that the two are a natural fit.

IFS work can complement the work you do on your Procrastination Pattern using this book. IFS would help you to experientially access the motivations and childhood origins behind this pattern and to heal and transform the pattern. Then your homework practice on developing your Work Confidence Capacity would be even more effective. If you want to experience the profoundest and most lasting change in your pattern, I recommend that you practice IFS with your Procrastination Part as described below.

The IFS Model

IFS enables you to understand each of the *parts* of your psyche, sometimes called *subpersonalities*. Think of them as little people inside you. Each has its own perspective, feelings, memories, goals, and motivations. And sometimes they are at odds with each other. For example, one part of you might be trying to lose weight, and another part might want to eat whatever you want. We all have many different parts, such as the procrastinator, the lover, the inner critic, the lonely child, the rebel, the caretaker, and so on.

If you have the Procrastination Pattern, there is a part of you that avoids dealing with certain situations. You can use IFS to work on your Procrastination Part as well as any other patterns you have.

IFS recognizes that we all have child parts that are in pain, which are called *exiles*. These correspond to the wounds in the Pattern System. The parts that try to keep us from feeling this pain are called *protectors*, which correspond to the patterns.

Most important, IFS recognizes that we all have a true *Self*, which is our core healthy place or spiritual center. IFS has some innovative and easy ways to access Self. You get to know your parts and develop trusting relationships with them from the place of Self, which then leads to healing and transformation of those parts.

The IFS Process with Your Procrastination Part

IFS is an experiential therapy. You don't just get insight into your parts. You actually go inside, contact them, and have conversations with them.

What follows is a brief description of how you would do IFS with your Procrastination Part. It is just an overview to give you an idea of how the process works. The actual procedure is much more detailed and specialized. We don't expect you to be able to do IFS by reading this brief description. You will need to learn how to engage in the IFS process using my book *Self-Therapy* or courses, or by going into individual therapy with an IFS therapist (see Appendix C).

First you access your Procrastination Part experientially. You might feel it emotionally, or hear its words, or get a mental image of what it looks like. Then you access Self so that you are separate from your Procrastination Part and have a place to stand from which to connect with it. You make sure that you are open to getting to know it from its own perspective rather than judging it or wanting to get rid of it.

Then you ask it to tell you what it is trying to accomplish for you by keeping you focused on avoiding things. You want to know what it is afraid would happen if it allowed you to take decisive action. This helps you to recognize the exile (wounded inner child part) that it is protecting.

This conversation will give you a good sense of how the Procrastination Part is trying to protect you, even if that protection isn't really needed anymore. This allows you to appreciate its efforts on your behalf, and your appreciation helps the Procrastination Part to trust you.

You ask the Procrastination Part for permission to work with the exile it is protecting. Then you get to know that child part and find out what happened when you were young to cause that part to be so afraid and wounded. You witness these memories in an experiential way (you may or may not know them already)—that is, you see them in a mental movie of your past. Then you enter the childhood scene and give that little child what he or she needed back then. Or you protect the wounded child part from being harmed. You might also take that part out of that harmful or painful childhood situation and into your present life, where he or she will be safe and can be connected to you and receive your love and caring.

You help the exile to release the pain and fear that he or she has been carrying all these years. Once this is done, your Procrastination Part won't feel the need to protect the exile anymore, so it can now relax and stop trying to make you avoid tasks and projects. Then you will be able to have the confidence in your work that you want.

My book *Self-Therapy* describes in detail how to use IFS to work through any psychological issue. See www.selflead-ership.org for detailed information about IFS and professional training in the Model. My colleagues and I also offer courses in which you can learn how to use IFS to work on yourself and do peer counseling with other people from the course. See Appendix C for IFS resources.

Conclusion

I hope this book will help you to transform your Procrastination Pattern so you can have the work confidence, stick-to-it-iveness, and productivity you desire. In order for this to happen, it is important that you fully engage in the practice of creating Work Confidence in Chapter 7. Reading this material and understanding yourself is an important step, but most people need to consciously work on putting this into practice in their lives.

You also may need to work on other patterns of yours in order to fully let go of Procrastination. Your Procrastination Pattern may be linked to a Perfectionist Pattern, a Defiant Pattern, or one of the others that are mentioned in the book. You may be able to create the Work Confidence you want by only focusing on your Procrastination Pattern, but you might need to do more to achieve success. If this is the case, read other books in this series or find other ways to work on those patterns.

Don't become discouraged if your pattern doesn't transform right away. Personal growth isn't a simple, easy process, despite what some self-help books would have you believe. Letting go of a deep-seated problem takes time and effort and a commitment to work on yourself.

Personal growth is an exciting journey, with twists and turns, painful revelations, unexpected insights, profound shifts, and an ever-deepening sense of self-awareness and mastery. I hope that this book contributes to your personal evolution and the deep satisfaction that comes from living a life of ease and productivity.

APPENDIX A

The Pattern System[SM]

The Procrastination Pattern and the Accomplishment Dimension that contains it are just one small part of the overall Pattern System. You can use the Pattern System to obtain a complete map of your psyche. You will be able to see your strengths and your defenses, your places of pain and how you compensate for them. You'll come to understand the structure of your inner conflicts and see where you are ready to grow. The Pattern System makes clear what you need to explore next in order to resolve the issues that are most important to you.

The goal of working with the Pattern System is to live from your *True Self,* which is who you naturally are when you aren't operating from patterns and when you have developed skills for healthy relating and functioning. Work Confidence is one aspect of the True Self.

A more advanced goal is to live from your *Higher Self,* which is your spiritual ground and is the integration of the higher capacities, including Higher Accomplishment.

Personal Dimensions in the Pattern System

The Accomplishment Dimension is just one of the personal dimensions in the Pattern System, each containing at least two patterns and two capacities. The following are brief descriptions of some of them:

Self-Esteem. Do you feel good about yourself, or do you constantly judge yourself? Do you accept yourself as you are? Do you try to prop up your self-esteem with pride? How do you deal with improving yourself?

Accomplishment. Are you confident in working on and accomplishing tasks? Do you procrastinate? Do you push or judge yourself to try to get things done or to achieve, or can you accomplish with ease?

Pleasure. How do you deal with food, drink, sex, and other bodily pleasures? Do you indulge in harmful ways? Do you control yourself rigidly to avoid doing that? Do you bounce back and forth between overindulging and castigating yourself?

Some further personal dimensions are:

- Action
- Change
- Hope
- Excellence
- Decision
- Risk
- Rationality/Emotion

Each of these dimensions has the same structure as the Accomplishment Dimension. There will be a book on each of the patterns in each dimension. Visit http://personal-growth-programs.com/pattern-system/pattern-system-series to see if they are available.

Interpersonal Dimensions in the Pattern System

The Pattern System also deals with a variety of interpersonal patterns. The following are brief descriptions of some of them:

Conflict. How do you deal with differences of opinion as well as desires, disagreements, judgment, anger, and fights? Do you use avoidance tactics? Do you become angry, blaming, or defensive? Can you communicate your concerns without judgment and own your part in a problem? Do you become frightened or feel bad about yourself? Can you bring up conflicts and set limits on attacks?

Social. How do you relate to people socially? Are you outgoing or shy, scared or confident in reaching out to people or making conversation? Are you self-effacing or charming, attention seeking or avoiding? Are you overly oriented toward performance in the way you relate to others, or are you more genuine?

Care. How do you balance your needs versus other people's needs? Do you end up taking care of others rather than yourself? Do people tell you that you don't show enough care or concern for them?

Intimacy. Do you avoid intimacy, need it too much, fear it, love it? Can you be autonomous in an intimate relationship without denying your needs? Do you get overly dependent in relationships, or can you support yourself?

Power. How do you deal with power in your relationships? Do you give in too easily to others or try too hard to please them? Do you need to be in control? Do you feel as though you must stand up for yourself against people you view as dominating? Do you frustrate others without realizing why? Can you assert yourself? Can you work with people in a spirit of cooperation?

Anger and Strength. How do you deal with self-protection and assertiveness in situations that can bring up anger? Do you dump your anger on people? Do you disown your anger and therefore lose your strength? Can you be centered and communicate clearly when you are angry? Can you be strong and forceful without being reactive?

Trust. Are you usually trusting of people, or do you easily get suspicious? Can you perceive when someone isn't trustworthy, or are you gullible?

Some additional interpersonal dimensions are:

- Honesty
- Evaluation
- Responsibility

Each of these dimensions has the same structure as the Accomplishment Dimension. There will be a book on each of the patterns in each dimension. Visit http://personal-growth-programs.com/pattern-system/pattern-system-series to see which ones are available now.

Wounds

The following are the main wounds:

Harm Wounds

1. Deficiency Wound
2. Betrayal Wound
3. Violation Wound
4. Shame Wound

5. Attack Wound

6. Powerless Wound

7. Exploitation Wound

Rejection Wounds

1. Need Wound

2. Unlovable Wound

3. Deficiency Wound

Other Wounds

1. Dead Wound

2. Fear-of-Disaster Wound

3. Chaos Wound

4. Hopeless Wound

5. Self-Doubt Wound

Motivations

The following are some of the important motivations:

- Fear of Harm

- Fear of Rejection

- Fear of Losing Yourself

- Attempt to Stop Harm

- Attempt to Stop Pain

- Attempt to Get Connection

- Fear of Success

- Fear of Failure

- Opposition to a Parent

An Open-Ended System

The Pattern System is open-ended. We sometimes add new patterns, subpatterns, capacities, and dimensions, or even new types of patterns. We welcome input from other people in developing the Pattern System further. See http://thepatternsystem.wikispaces.com for a fuller outline of the system.

Definitions of Terms

Dimension. An area of psychological functioning (e.g., power, intimacy, or self-esteem) that contains certain patterns and capacities that deal with similar issues.

Healthy Capacity. A way of behaving or feeling that makes your life productive, connected, and happy. An aspect of the True Self.

Higher Self. Your spiritual ground and the integration of your higher capacities.

Inner Champion. An aspect of yourself that supports and encourages you and helps you feel good about yourself. It is the magic bullet for dealing with the negative impact of the Inner Critic.

Inner Critic. A part of you that judges you, demeans you, and pushes you to do things. It tends to make you feel bad about yourself.

Interpersonal Pattern. A pattern that involves interpersonal relating.

Life Situation. A situation that is coming up in the next week or two in which you will have the opportunity to practice creating a healthy capacity instead of prolonging a pattern.

Motivation. A kind of underlying intention (e.g., fear of harm or desire for approval) that drives a pattern.

Pattern. A way of behaving or feeling that is a problem for you or others (e.g., being dependent, controlling, or judgmental). A pattern tends to be too rigid, extreme, dysfunctional, or inappropriate for the situation you are in.

Polarization. A dynamic in which two patterns are fighting each other to determine how you behave or relate to others.

Taskmaster Pattern. A pattern that involves pushing yourself unmercifully to overwork, often in an attempt to be very successful, and judging yourself harshly whenever you don't.

True Self. Who you naturally are when you aren't operating from patterns and when you have developed skills for healthy relating and functioning. The healthy capacities are aspects of the True Self.

Wound. A harmful or traumatic way you were treated, usually in childhood (e.g., being neglected, hit, or dismissed).

Resources

Books

Self-Therapy, by Jay Earley. How to do Internal Family Systems (IFS) sessions on your own or with a partner. Also a manual of the IFS method that can be used by therapists.

Self-Therapy for Your Inner Critic, by Jay Earley and Bonnie Weiss. Applies IFS to working with Inner Critic parts.

Resolving Inner Conflict, by Jay Earley. How to work with polarization using IFS.

Working with Anger in IFS, by Jay Earley. How to work with too much anger or disowned anger using IFS.

Activating Your Inner Champion Instead of Your Inner Critic, by Jay Earley and Bonnie Weiss. How to bring forth your Inner Champion to deal with attacks from your Inner Critic.

Embracing Intimacy, by Jay Earley. How to work through blocks that keep you from having the intimacy you want in your love relationship.

Letting Go of Perfectionism, by Jay Earley and Bonnie Weiss. How to work through fears that lead to perfectionism so you can have more ease and perspective in your life.

A series of Pattern System books similar to this one will be published over the next few years. A list of the currently available Pattern System books will be maintained and updated at http://www.personal-growth-programs.com/pattern-system-series.

Updates for this book. Visit http://www.personal-growth-programs.com/taking-action-owners to register yourself as an owner of this book. You will receive an updated version of the book whenever it is improved. You will also be notified about each new book in the series as it comes out.

Courses

My colleagues and I teach telephone courses on Perfectionism, Procrastination, and many of the other topics of the Pattern System books. We also teach telephone courses on IFS for the general public. My website (with Bonnie Weiss) http://www.personal-growth-programs.com has the details.

Websites and Applications

My IFS website (with Bonnie Weiss), http://www.personal-growth-programs.com, contains popular and professional articles on IFS and its application to various psychological issues. You can also sign up for our email list to receive future articles and notifications of upcoming courses and groups.

My personal website, http://www.jayearley.com, contains more of my writings and information about my psychotherapy practice, including my therapy groups.

Our other website, http://www.psychemaps.com, contains a questionnaire to determine which of the seven types of Inner Critics you have and a program to profile your Inner Critic and Inner Champion.

The Procrastination Online Community (http://www.personal-growth-programs.com/connect) is for people who are reading this book and would like to support each other in letting go of Procrastination. It is part of a larger online community of people who are working on various aspects of their personal growth and healing through our books, websites, and programs.

The Pattern System website, http://thepatternsystem.wikispaces.com, contains an outline of the latest version.

The Center for Self-Leadership is the official IFS organization. Its website, http://www.selfleadership.org, contains IFS articles, trainings, workshops, and a list of IFS therapists.

Books and Booklets by
Jay Earley, PhD

The IFS Series
Self-Therapy
Self-Therapy for Your Inner Critic (with Bonnie Weiss)
Resolving Inner Conflict
Working with Anger in IFS
Negotiating for Self-Leadership**

The Pattern System Series
Embracing Intimacy
Letting Go of Perfectionism (with Bonnie Weiss)
Taking Action
A Pleaser No Longer**
Beyond Caretaking**

The Inner Critic Series (with Bonnie Weiss)
Self-Therapy for Your Inner Critic
Activating Your Inner Champion
in Place of Your Inner Critic
Letting Go of Perfectionism

Other Books
Interactive Group Therapy
Transforming Human Culture
Inner Journeys

**Forthcoming

Manufactured by Amazon.ca
Bolton, ON